# THUD!

by
Mark Weakland

illustrated by
Christian Cornia

# Wile E. Coyote
### Experiments with
# FORCES and MOTION

CAPSTONE PRESS
a capstone imprint

Published in 2014 by Capstone Press
A Capstone Imprint
1710 Roe Crest Drive
North Mankato, Minnesota 56003
www.capstonepub.com

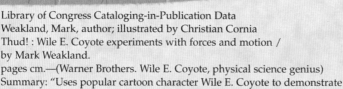

Library of Congress Cataloging-in-Publication Data
Weakland, Mark, author; illustrated by Christian Cornia
Thud! : Wile E. Coyote experiments with forces and motion /
by Mark Weakland.
pages cm.—(Warner Brothers. Wile E. Coyote, physical science genius)
Summary: "Uses popular cartoon character Wile E. Coyote to demonstrate
science concepts involved with forces and motion."—Provided by publisher.
Includes bibliographical references and index.
ISBN 978-1-4765-4221-8 (library binding)
ISBN 978-1-4765-5212-5 (paperback)
1. Kinematics—Juvenile literature. 2. Kinematics—Experiments—Juvenile literature. 3. Force
and energy—Experiments—Juvenile literature. 4. Science projects—Juvenile literature. 5. Wile
E. Coyote (Fictitious character)—Juvenile literature. I. Warner Bros. II. Title. III. Title: Wile E.
Coyote experiments with forces and motion. IV. Title: Experiments with forces and motion.
QC137.52.W43 2014
531.112—dc23                                                          2013037011

Editorial Credits
Aaron Sautter, editor; Lori Bye, designer; Laura Manthe, production specialist


Cover Artist: Andrés Martínez Ricci


Capstone Press thanks Joanne K. Olson, Associate Professor of Science Education at
Iowa State University for her help in creating this book.

# Table of Contents

# Flying with Force

Poor Wile E. Coyote. If only he could catch that tasty Road Runner. From rolling rocks to rocket sleds, his crazy schemes set all sorts of things into motion. But his plans never seem to work. If Wile E. just understood the science of forces and motion, he might nab that speedy bird.

### Coyote
(Hungrius carnivorii)

mass—the amount of material in an object
accelerate—to increase the speed of a moving object

Whether sitting still or speeding down the road, Wile E. and Road Runner must both obey the laws of motion. These laws can be summed up as three general rules:

# The Three Laws of Motion

1. An object at rest will stay at rest until a force moves it. Similarly, an object in motion will stay in motion unless an opposing force stops it.
2. An object's speed increases or decreases based on its **mass** and the forces acting on it.
3. Every force has an equal and opposite force.

OUCH !

The laws of motion direct how Wile E. moves and how quickly he **accelerates**. They also determine how hard he hits when he crashes into a telephone pole. Sometimes the laws of motion can hurt! Let's take a closer look at some of Wile E.'s crazy schemes and discover why his ideas go so wrong.

**Road Runner**

(Speedius birdius)

5

In the late 1600s, Sir Isaac Newton was one of the first scientists to study motion. He watched objects in nature at rest and in motion. Then he used mathematics to explain what he observed. From his studies Newton developed new ideas that helped describe how and why objects move. Over time, Newton's ideas came to be known as the Three Laws of Motion.

Newton's first law states that objects at rest tend to stay at rest. In other words, when Wile E. sits in his lawn chair, he'll stay there until a force moves him. The law also says that objects in motion tend to stay in motion. So when Road Runner zooms by, he'll keep moving until an opposing force makes him stop.

TWANG

Newton's second law says that an object's speed increases or decreases based on its mass and the forces acting on it. For example, Road Runner has a certain mass. While running, he needs to add a certain amount of force to his legs if he wants to run faster.

Finally, Newton's third law states that forces all have an equal and opposite force. If a giant boulder slams down on Wile E.'s seesaw, the other end will spring up with equal force. Wile E. should have thought about Newton's third law before dropping that boulder!

# Chapter 1: Moving into Motion

## Setting Objects in Motion

Road Runner is in a state of constant motion. To catch him, Wile E. needs to get himself moving too. In other words, he needs to exert a force. A force, which is a push or a pull, is what makes an object move. Newton's First Law of Motion tells us about **inertia**. This idea says that an object at rest, such as a coyote, will stay that way unless a force acts on him.

What kind force will set Wile E. into motion? Wile E. can force his legs to push against the ground. When his legs push down, the ground pushes back with equal force. The ground pushes against his feet to move him forward.

inertia—the tendency of an object to remain either at rest or in motion unless affected by an outside force

Unfortunately for Wile E., his scrawny legs can't exert enough force to catch up to Road Runner.

# Stopping an Object

Wile E. runs fast, but he'll need more than leg force to catch Road Runner. He can get a boost from Acme's Super Spring Sneakers. With every step, the force of his muscles combines with the force of the sneaker springs.

According to Newton's First Law of Motion, the inertia of Wile E.'s forward motion will continue until another force acts on him. In other words, he'll keep springing forward until something makes him stop.

BOING!

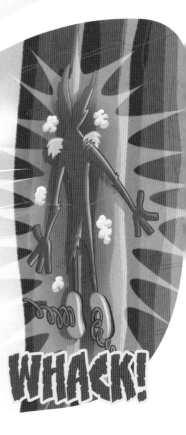

Road Runner can use the force of his legs to stop. But Wile E. has a problem. With all the Super Spring force behind him, he can't stop very easily.

WHACK!

Only a strong opposing force can stop Wile E.'s forward motion. Unfortunately for him, a rock wall provides the force needed. Ouch!

# Chapter 2: Going Against Gravity

## The Force of Gravity

In a land filled with canyons and cliffs, it's wise to keep your feet on the ground. Wile E. must not realize that **gravity** can ruin even the best-laid plans.

Gravity is the force that constantly pulls objects toward the Earth's center. When Wile E. is standing on the ground, gravity isn't a problem. But it becomes a problem when he tries to climb upside down on a high rock ledge. There's no way to get rid of gravity's downward pull. Wile E. can only hold on tight and hope to overcome it.

**gravity**—a force that pulls objects with mass together; gravity pulls objects down toward the center of Earth

gravity

Gravity's force is forever trying to pull resting bodies into motion. Wile E.'s grip may be strong, but it's not enough to overcome gravity's downward pull. Poor Wile E. never realized the gravity of his situation.

MEEP MEEP

FREE BIRD SEED

# Counteracting Gravity

To counteract gravity's pull, Wile E. needs a strong opposing force. His hands aren't strong enough to provide the force he needs. But Wile E. Coyote, "Science Genius," always has a plan. He's going to try his new Acme Super Suction Cups.

gravity

Suction cups provide the force Wile E. needs to overcome gravity. They stick to a surface by using the force of air **pressure**. But Wile E. has forgotten an important fact. As gravity pulls on him, it also pulls on the rock ledge he's clinging to. When the rock cracks, gravity brings everything crashing down.

pressure—a force that pushes or pulls on something

But at least Wile E. won't fall forever. Soon the canyon floor will provide a force to stop his downward motion. Then Wile E. and the falling rock will come to rest.

gravity

OUCH!!

force

# Lift and Air Resistance

It is possible to overcome gravity's pull and stay in the air for long periods of time. Wile E. knows that birds and airplanes beat gravity every day. And he thinks a coyote can too.

Wile E. tries using a pair of wings to get the lifting force he needs to defeat gravity. The wings' shape causes air to flow quickly over the top and more slowly along the bottom. The difference in airflow creates high pressure on the bottom of the wings and lower pressure above them. The high pressure pushes up on the wings to force them and Wile E. into the sky.

Of course, if the wings are damaged, they won't work correctly. No wings means no lift. And no lift means gravity will pull Wile E. to the ground. Sorry, Wile E.!

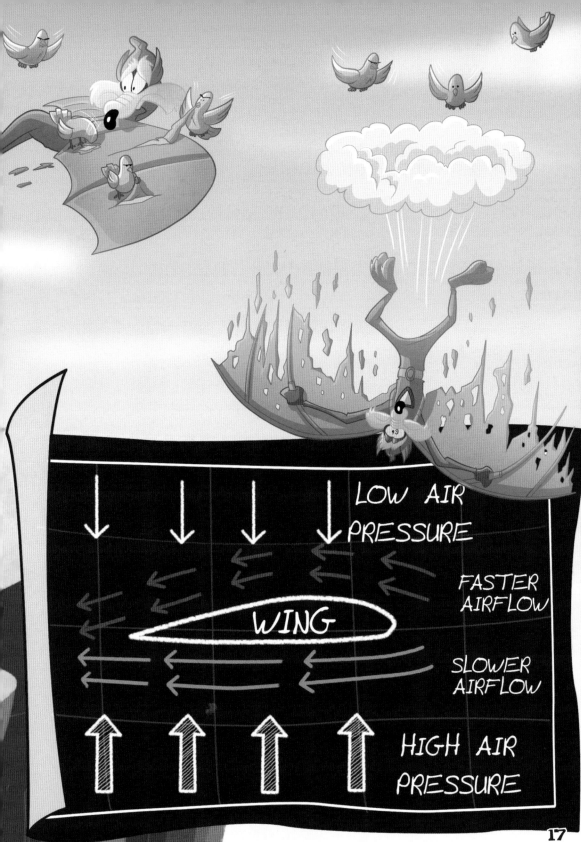

LOW AIR
PRESSURE

FASTER
AIRFLOW

WING

SLOWER
AIRFLOW

HIGH AIR
PRESSURE

# Chapter 3: Momentous Moments

## Acceleration

Wile E. hasn't had much luck so far. To match Road Runner's speed, he needs to accelerate quickly. Wile E. thinks his new Acme Super Rocket Car will help him do just that!

Newton's Second Law of Motion can help Wile E. determine how much acceleration he needs. The law says that acceleration is the amount of force needed to move an object with a certain mass. In this case the objects are Wile E. and his rocket car. The amount of acceleration needed to catch Road Runner depends on the total mass of Wile E. and the car. Other forces acting on the car also affect its acceleration.

When the rocket engine applies a strong force to the car, it moves forward very quickly. As Wile E. increases the engine's power, more force is applied to the car's tires. This in turn causes the car to move forward faster and faster. In other words, it accelerates.

Acceleration is thrilling, but it can be risky. With too much of it, Wile E. could zoom past Road Runner and head straight into trouble. He also needs to remember Newton's First Law—objects in motion tend to stay in motion.

# Moving with Momentum

Lots of acceleration leads to lots of speed. As Wile E. is about to learn, lots of speed can be dangerous. Like any moving object, a speeding rocket car has **momentum**. Momentum can be thought of as how difficult it is to stop a moving object. The more mass an object has, the more difficult it is to stop. Wile E.'s rocket car has a lot of mass. Combine that mass with high speed, and the rocket car has a lot of momentum.

Only a strong opposing force can stop a heavy object with a lot of momentum. Wile E.'s parachute can't provide enough force to stop the car. Can sagebrush or cactuses provide the force he needs?

momentum—the amount of force in a moving object
determined by the object's mass and speed

# Changing Direction

Wile E. claims to be a genius, but he must have forgotten another part of Newton's First Law of Motion. The First Law says that a moving object keeps moving in the same direction until a force acts on it.

Road Runner can change direction by changing the angle of his legs and feet. As his legs push sideways against the road, they change the direction of his body. This sideways force works the same as the front wheels of a car. When a car's front tires are turned by the steering wheel, the sideways force changes the direction of the car.

But Wile E.'s Desert Surfer lacks something important—a steering wheel! He has no way to turn its front wheels and change its direction. The Desert Surfer will keep moving forward in a straight line until another force acts on it. Time to hit the brakes, Wile E.!

# Friction

Uh, oh. Wile E.'s Desert Surfer is missing more than a steering wheel. It has no brakes! Fortunately, the force of **friction** seems to be slowing it down.

Friction is a force that counteracts motion. Friction slows objects down as they rub against one another. As the wheels of the Surfer rub against the ground, the force slows their rotation and the Surfer's speed. But the amount of friction between the wheels and the ground is small. The speed is reduced only a little.

ENTERING
**PRICKLY PEAR**
POPULATION   0

friction—a force created when two objects rub together; friction slows down objects

However, Wile E. can create more friction by leaning back to drag the Surfer's back end on the ground. When there is a lot of friction, moving objects slow down quickly.

SKREEECH

But friction also produces heat. This is why your hands get warm when you rub them together quickly. Wile E. is really feeling the heat now!

# Chapter 4

# Lights ... Camera ... Action ... Reaction:

## Action and Reaction

Wile E. doesn't realize it, but he's about to experience Newton's third and most famous law of motion. The law states that for every force, there is an equal and opposite force.

Wile E. is getting ready to fire an Acme Mobile Cannon at Road Runner. But nobody told him about the gun's **recoil**. The recoil is the opposing force that matches the forward momentum of the cannonball. In a heavy gun like a cannon, the recoil force is transferred from the cannon's mount to the ground. But Wile E. forgot to lock the cannon's wheels. When he fires it, the cannon will roll backward as the cannonball flies forward.

recoil—the kickback of a gun when firing

Wile E. just learned that standing behind a cannon isn't the safest spot. Don't blame Newton, Wile E. He didn't make the laws of motion—he only described them!

BLAM

# Tricky Laws of Motion

Wile E. has worked hard on his latest scheme. Look closely and you'll see Newton's laws of motion at work. But Wile E. still hasn't learned much about them. When he sets the boulder into motion, its mass creates momentum that is difficult to stop. The boulder's action causes a reaction that Wile E. doesn't expect.

Figuring out forces and motion is tricky business. One mistake can ruin even the best plans. Will Wile E. ever be able to catch that speedy Road Runner? If he ever wants to succeed, he'll have to study the laws of forces and motion more closely in the future.

# Glossary

**accelerate** (ak-SEL-uh-rayt)—to increase the speed of a moving object

**friction** (FRIK-shuhn)—a force created when two objects rub together; friction slows down objects

**gravity** (GRAV-uh-tee)—a force that pulls objects together; gravity pulls objects down toward the center of Earth

**inertia** (in-UR-shuh)—the tendency of an object to remain either at rest or in motion unless affected by an outside force

**mass** (MASS)—the amount of material in an object

**momentum** (moh-MEN-tuhm)—the amount of force in a moving object determined by the object's mass and speed

**pressure** (PRESH-ur)—a force that pushes or pulls on something

**recoil** (RI-koil)—the kickback of a gun when firing

# Read More

Biskup, Agnieszka. *The Gripping Truth about Forces and Motion.* LOL Physical Science. North Mankato, Minn.: Capstone Press, 2013.

Boothroyd, Jennifer. *Forces.* First Physics. Minneapolis: Lerner Publications Co., 2011.

Weakland, Mark A. *Zombies and Forces and Motion.* Monster Science. Mankato, Minn.: Capstone Press, 2012.

# Internet Sites

FactHound offers a safe, fun way to find Internet sites related to this book. All of the sites on FactHound have been researched by our staff.

Here's all you do:

Visit *www.facthound.com*

Type in this code: 9781476542218

# Index